4TH AND LONG

Trusting God to Move the Chains

Clarence (Bobby Lemon) Lemond

By God's Grace
Publishing Company, LLC

ACKNOWLEDGMENTS

I give praise, honor, and glory to my Lord and Savior, Jesus Christ, who has graced me through my trials and tribulations.

To my wife, Wanda Lemond, for being my strong supporter. Your words of encouragement, prayer, and love have inspired me more than you will ever know. I love you.

Thanks to my six true friends who have stuck by me through thick and thin. First, John Taylor, who is gone to be with the Lord, John set the bar high on suffering quietly, giving God the glory. Next, Vernon Nash, Sydney Ross, and I have been praying online two to three times a week for about 30 years. Donnelley came on board about 8 to 10 years ago. Rodney Schells and Lee Costello round out the breakfast group. A true friend is invaluable. Words cannot express my appreciation and love for you guys.

To my daughter from God, Joyce Smith of By God's Grace Publishing LLC, thank you for supporting the vision God has given me.

FROM THE HEART OF THE AUTHOR

This book was written for those who are like me and who have fallen short of their God-given assignment.

4th and Long: Trusting God to Move the Chains

CONTENTS

INTRODUCTION

Life is like a football game: four downs to get a first down. Four quarters to win the game. The regulation gives you three downs to make a first down, and if you are inefficient, you must use the fourth down. You do not want to use the fourth down because there is no room for error. You have four quarters to win the game; you do not want to wait until the fourth quarter to try to win.

CHAPTER 1
WE ALL HAVE A PURPOSE

God has placed us all on this earth for a specific purpose. I can't accomplish your purpose, and you can't accomplish mine.

I was lying in a hospital bed at North Western Memorial Hospital with pneumonia for the second time, fighting to stay alive, fighting with all I knew, feeling for sure I was transitioning, not truly realizing I had no control over whether I would live or die.

Still, it is God who is in control. I came to myself and asked God to forgive me. You see, God is in control of my past, present, and future. Then, I felt God's presence and saw His presence in my bed. I stopped sinking, and God assured me I would live. Afterward, I asked God to forgive me for not wholly trusting Him despite all the years I had been saved. I had been actively involved in various roles—teaching Sunday School, training teachers, serving as a department superintendent, acting as a general superintendent, and preaching for 15 years. Strangely enough, my poor wife had just left my bedside to return home after seeking support at the Sunday School, urging them to pray for her husband because she believed Satan was attempting to steal him away. My poor wife hadn't slept since I was admitted to the hospital.

She had a CD in her car that her sister had given her about two months prior. She had not opened it. The Holy Spirit told her it was time to listen to it. She put the CD in the player while sitting in the parking garage. She listened to the CD by Kim Stratten all the way home. After a hot shower, my wife fell asleep and got some much-needed rest. She had not had a night of restful sleep; this was the first time since I had been hospitalized. Not knowing my plight, my wife came into my hospital room the following day looking like a young bride. Seeing my beautiful wife made me feel energized enough to rise out of my hospital bed and go home right then.

Back to me: after my encounter with my Lord, I slept so soundly. I did not remember the nurse coming into my room, taking all the tubes out, or anything else. After my wife told me why she looked so fresh and beautiful, I knew God had ministered to us both. All this was happening at the same time. I knew then that God was calming her spirit, assuring me that I would live and not die to declare His work.

By the way, she had never looked so beautiful.

This made me reflect on my life and my capacity for care. Thus was born 4th and Long. I realized I was in the 4th quarter of my life, which is the last quarter, and I had much ground to make up. A lot to get down to and not a lot of time to get it done. After having a kidney transplant in 1998, after having cancer in my native kidneys in 2007 and having them removed, God did not allow cancer to affect the transplanted kidney. I had to reevaluate my life. I came to realize that the pain and suffering had caused me to get on the right track. You see when you are born, that is the kick-off. What we must focus on is from goal post to goal post. What are we going to do between the two goalposts? The enemy attacks are but an exercise for the believer.

CHAPTER 2
YOU ARE VICTORIOUS

God's plan and your destiny. Life is similar to a football game in four quarters. To win the game, don't wait until the fourth quarter to get it done. From the kick–off, when you become born again, until you transition. Remember, your troubles come to make you stronger. The enemy attacks are but an exercise for the believers.

I was born the 10th child to Rufus and Rosie Lee Lemons in West Hermondale, Missouri. My father and his brother, Levi Lemons, shared adjoining farms. They were both preachers.

Not only was working on the farm hard, but walking to and from school was also tough. If I had to do it over again, I would. We had to learn to use kerosene lamps until I was in the 8th grade. The school was enjoyable because it gave you a break from the hard farm work. I excelled in math and was great at reading and spelling.

After high school, I joined the Army in 1964–67. My first assignment was the 101st Airborne Division, Ft. Campbell, KY; I was jumping out of airplanes. Imagine a poor country boy who had never been on a plane before. After that, I was shipped off to Turkey, where I was a Nuclear Weapons Specialist. I was promoted to SGT E5 and placed over a section. I assembled the weapons; most young soldiers were afraid to deal with nuclear weapons. The name intimidated most of us. We were so young and green.

I got out of the Army in May 1967. I got my first job at Western Electric. I worked there from 1967 until I was laid off in 1979. I was laid off for a couple of years. Then, in 1981, I landed a low-paying job at Astra Photo. It didn't matter that the pay was low. I had four children to care for. "But God." I did not know that because I was not too proud to accept this low-paying job, God would turn that job into the greatest blessing. God gave me and my family favor with the owner, and he blessed me with that job.

God will not leave you nor forsake you *(Hebrews 13:5 NIV).* God turned that low-paying job into a managerial position. In 1996, I had to go on dialysis and didn't lose any pay. I received my kidney in 1998. After about two years of dialysis, my wife and I were told that the kidney would last, at best, ten to twelve years. God had something to say about that; it lasted three weeks short of twenty-one years. I don't know what I would have done or how I would have made it without the Lord and my loving wife by my side.

Oh, yes—my wife. We met when she was seventeen years old. She loved me with her whole heart. Therefore, I had to choose her. She stuck with me through sickness and in health. We have been together for some 55 years and still love one another. Like I told my sons, we are still in love.

I started this project in 2011. Procrastination stretched it until 2022 because I am too hard on myself. You can't force writing; it has to come to you, and you have to be diligent.

I always knew God had His hands on me, but I restrained them. I thought my plan was better for me. My first calling was in 1986 at Christ Tabernacle MB Church under the leadership of the late Rev. Milton Brunson. I became a Sunday school teacher. I later became the instructor for the young men at the Timothy Club. I also became chairman of the deacon board. In 1997, after accepting my calling, which I believe was the second time, God, in His infinite mercy, allowed me another chance.

CHAPTER 3
GETTING IT TOGETHER

relocated to the Apostolic Faith Church at 38th and Indiana under the leadership of Bishop Horace E. Smith. There, I became a teacher and teacher's trainer, department superintendent, and general superintendent. I received my teacher's training certification from the Pentecostal Assembly of the World (PAW). Right out of class, I was chosen to teach Growing Towards Spiritual Maturity, the greatest blessing ever. I was forced to learn fast. I was thrown into a class with mostly ministers and evangelists established in the church. But God came through.

Still, the church did not know I was a minister. After so long, I was comfortable hiding. I began to turn over in my mind: how many people perished might not have been saved. I realized I had to do what I was called to: bring those out of darkness into the light. Sometimes, we are slothful in getting it together. I was sitting under the best and most powerful preaching and teachings, I believe, on the planet. Sometimes, we want muscles without exercise. I had been praying for urgency and energy. I had, but failed to connect. Some things only come through fasting and praying. God will not accept excuses. My God will meet all your needs according to the riches of His glory in Christ Jesus. *(Philippians 4:19 NIV)*

Let us not mistake this for material stuff. God will supply all we need to do the work He puts us here to do. At first, I did not have a clue about the seriousness of God's call on my life. I thought God was doing so much, and I was doing so much. Being at church heavily and teaching The Word, I did not realize it was all God and none of me. What if I had gotten it sooner? My GOD!

God is not slack concerning His promises. He'll bring it to pass, and now there is no time to waste. The race is not given to the swift nor the battle to the strong, but to those who endure to the end. *(Ecclesiastes 9:11, NIV)* No matter how long you live, your life can be divided into four quarters.

In football, you get three regular plays or downs to make a first down or 10 yards. You don't want to have to use the 4th down. Some people, as soon as they are saved, leave right out of the gate. Some procrastinate like me and find themselves with lots of yardage to make up. But don't despair; God is able to do exceeding and abundantly above all we can ask or think. *(Ephesians 3:20 KJV)* Since I started this journey of putting pen to paper, the enemy has tried his best to take me out.

After going back on dialysis in April 2019, in March 2020, I was diagnosed with lung cancer. For three days, I could not eat. Again, I came to myself, realizing whose I am. I prayed a short prayer: "Lord, you told me that when the enemy would come in like a flood, Your Spirit would lift a standard against him." Within 30 minutes, my appetite returned.

Four days later, the doctor called with good news, and I told her I knew it was coming. She said we are looking at your x-rays, and you are a candidate for surgery. I shouted, "Glory to God!"

She said, "We can take 25% of your lung, and you should be okay." They took half of the left lung, but who's measuring? No chemo, no radiation. In February 2021, I bragged about God, telling my prayer partners after they called me the Miracle Man that it does not matter what the devil tries to do to me as long as I know to give God the glory. Four days later, I could not stand up and walk. I had a cerebral stroke, but God! After three days, I was out of the hospital with no side effects.

I just want to stop right here and say GLORY! I think my God has left me in the race. I don't believe it is the will of God that we measure our lives by the parable of the vineyard or the thief on the cross; who is to say you will get that chance?

I thank my God, who gives us chance after chance.

I also believe the earth may be in the last quarter of its existence. Forest fires continue to burn year-round. Devastation by hurricanes, tornadoes, COVID-19, and drugs is running rampant while the gangs are killing and terrorizing neighborhoods. Kids with guns are killing kids. Homosexuality is the new norm. Our government is widely divided. Anything one party wants, the other party strongly opposes.

Jesus said a house divided against itself should not stand. *(Matthew 12:25 NIV)* Jesus also spoke of the end times over 2000 years ago. We are much closer now. Therefore, with the things I have to do, I can't mess up the last play. I have to have a single-minded focus.

Taking a page out of a baseball player's method of stealing bases, he said that when he decided to go for a base, he had no intentions of returning to the base he left. So, he gave all he had to the base before him.

God has given and forgiven us many times and given us a new start. We put all our failures behind us and press forward. God requires us to be like a polished arrow, sharp and smooth, with no rust, so our aim is swift and true, hitting its mark with accuracy. Rust weighs down the arrow and causes it to veer off course. God wants us to be fresh and smooth. When we come before His people, prayer, studying, and meditation on His Word are essential; committing more time to fasting and praying will yield surprising revelations about what God has for your ministry. The word says, Commit your way to the Lord; trust in Him, and He will do this. *(Psalms 37:5 NIV)*

CHAPTER 4
GOD'S ASSURANCE

God promises to be with you in your lack. *I will be with you in your distress; I will be with you wherever you go.* You can count on God. Can God count on you?

This is my personal prayer. First, Lord, after You have been so faithful to me, let me never forget to seek Your face for all You have ordained me to do. Second, Lord, after You have been faithful in delivering on my requests, I will never forget my promises to

You. Please help me commit all my ways to You.

Only this will cause You to bring my life in line with Your desire and will. Lord, I am thankful for this day You have blessed me to see. I am beginning to understand how great You are and how every aspect of my life depends on You. I am so grateful to You, Lord, for allowing me to lie flat on my back for several days and to come close to transitioning, and You did not let it happen. Nor did You allow me to lose my faith for a fleeting moment. I was afraid of leaving my wife, children, and grandchildren, but You stepped in, lifted a standard against the enemy, and assured me I would live. I could see clearly that You were always in control. Lord, I pray today that You will help me redeem the times, maximize my efforts, and trust in You. Lord, those whom You love, You chasten. I thank You, God, for being a good father. AMEN.

I can't understand why some of us must get into the valley of despair before seeing Your hand clearly in our lives. One thing out of the many things I went through. This helped me see that I was way off course. We are often stuck in a place of comfort and ease or ritual. We have an appearance of holiness from the outside, but within, we are a rotten mess. In the valley, many of our options are taken away. Then, we really seek God's face. I can stop and shout. GLORY!

CHAPTER 5
UNDERSTANDING MY PURPOSE

Not only have I found myself in a fourth-down situation in life, but I also have lots of yardage to make up. I am on the 10th-yard line when I should be closer to the end zone or the finish line. Now to Him, who is able to do immeasurably more than all we ask or imagine, according to His power that is at work within us. *(Ephesians 3:20 NIV)*

Paul put it in more precise terms. "Forgetting what is behind and straining toward what is ahead, press on toward the goal to win the prize for which God has called me heavenward in Christ Jesus." *(Philippians 3:13-14 NIV)* We must choose to leave the world behind us. This is the only way God can use us fully for His purpose.

You see, we are in this world, but not of this world. We did not come from this world, and this world has nothing to offer us but to help the unsaved come out of darkness into the light of Jesus Christ. We have to put all of our failures behind us and look to Jesus, the author and finisher of our lives. God has forgiven me many times and given me a new start.

Well, I am old and don't have time for many more starts. I have been in this ministry for about 15 years. I have had many chances to move with God in a mighty way. I have become a teacher at Apostolic Faith Church under Bishop Horace E. Smith. God requires us to be like a polished arrow, sharp and smooth, with no rust, so our aim can be swift and true, hitting its mark with accuracy. Our issues are weighing down the rust.

It's not about us but about God. We are to be fresh daily when allowed to come before His people. Prayer, studying, and meditation are essential. Committing more time to fasting and praying will yield surprising revelations about what God has for your ministry. He says, Commit thy way unto the Lord; trust also in Him; He will bring you out.

God promises to be with you in your lack. I will be with you in your distress. I will be with you wherever you go. You can count on God. Can God count on you?

Many questions arise as my friends and I discuss the things happening in this world. One question is: when are we getting back to normal? News flash: Normal isn't coming back, but Jesus is.

Brother Hollis, a wise old man in my Sunday School class about 15 years or so ago, when I was general superintendent of the Sunday School, gave me a life-changing message when he told me one Sunday morning, "The bend in the road is not the end of the road unless you fail to turn." This life-changing quote causes you to look at trouble very differently. Trouble is just a bend in the road. Sometimes, you have no choice but to go with it or crash and burn.

With my list of health challenges, I never thought that I would make 76, but God.

Many are called, but few are chosen. *(Matthews 22:14 KJV)* You don't get to choose what God wants from you. Whatever it is, He will supply all you need to get the job done, which you can count on! Out of all of Jacob's twelve sons, the chosen one, Joseph, went through, as we say, hell and high waters. His brothers were jealous of him; he was sold into slavery; Potiphar's wife lied to him, and he was put in jail, but God raised him up. This means using whatever we are chosen to do. We should focus on bringing glory to God, not dwelling on ourselves and what we are going through.

God has promised not to leave us nor forsake us. We can have joy in our troubles if we keep our minds on the Lord. I heard a Christian say that Satan is relentless. So is God.

Joseph had a greater mission than his agenda—saving his family and God's nation of Israel. What joy it is to let your life bring glory to our God during this journey! We are going to make a lot of mistakes. As long as we confess our sins, He will pick us up repeatedly until we get it right. Our congressmen, our senators, our presidents, our governors, etc., will not endure sound doctrine and have turned the truth into a lie, which is their truth.

I am still learning daily not to be anxious about anything, but by prayer and supplication, I am letting all my requests be made known to God. The trying of our faith will make us better. I want my faith to be like when I pop the top of a can of soda. I never hesitate; I just pop the top and drink. Think about it—very few, if any, look down that little hole in the can before drinking. Think about it! Just as that cold drink will quench your thirst, so will God quench your needs and desires if you just trust Him.

If God did not allow or send us through trials and struggles, we would never experience His revealing, healing, or magnificent power, thus realizing He is the Great "I AM." We have experienced God differently during this pandemic. God has expanded people's minds through their desire to gather via video hookups. I remember how great this experience was when we could get together, as we had been doing it for years and took it for granted. Everyone experienced genuine love for one another.

Many times, we look at trouble, heartache, and pain as punishment. We have to look at it differently. God is steering us to our destiny. Otherwise, we need to make sure our lifestyle matches our calling. Many times in this walk, we can feel trapped; it's hard to continue, and we can't go back when we trust in God. You must trust Him and go forward, knowing the dying world depends on us to show them the way. Paul said, Who shall separate us from the love of Christ? Shall trouble or hardship or persecution or famine or nakedness or danger or sword? (*Romans 8:34–36 NIV*)

Paul was saying, *I would let nothing separate me from the love of God, I mean, nothing (Romans 8:35 KJV).* In case some might not understand these terms, as my mother used to say in plain English, losing your job? Losing your car? Losing your house? Broken personal relationships? Is someone talking about you? Losing your health? Nothing can separate me from the love of God through Christ Jesus.

CHAPTER 6
CONCLUSION OF THE MATTER

I am telling you what I know. There were times I felt like throwing in the towel. But the spirit of the Lord spoke to me and said, I will not die but live, and I will proclaim what the Lord has done. (*Psalms 118:17 NIV*)

I often reflect on my childhood. Growing up on a farm was always hard: hot in the summer, cold in the winter, and hard work. When my mom and dad, Rosie Lee Lemons and Rufus L. Lemons, gave you a job to do, there weren't any negotiations. I was promised a bike almost every year, only to find out we couldn't afford it. I felt betrayed and cheated for a long time until I grew up and found out that work seemed hard to the city guys. It was only a child's play for me.

Sometimes, it takes a while to appreciate hard work and obedience. If we walk in obedience to God, our work on earth will not be grievous. In this walk of faith, God will send you plenty of nuggets if you keep an open, prayerful mind.

One other nugget, a young minister, spoke at a gathering with one of the Elders. He was asked what his greatest fear was. His answer, "unrealized potential," says it all.

God gives us all the potential. It is up to us to bring it to realization.

After finding myself thanking God for the things He brought me out of, I realized that greater than that were the things He did not allow me to get into. I was prompted to write down my thoughts when I was in Northwestern Hospital with pneumonia for the second time in the same year, 2011.

I began to reflect on how short I had fallen in my godly assignment. In the fourth quarter of my life, there is much ground to make up.

What stage of life are you in? How are you doing on your assignment? Or have you identified your assignment?

I thank God for maturing me. For a long time, after she became a teenager, my daughter and I had a strained relationship. The conflict was her courting, and I wanted her to go to college. When I lost that battle, I still believed all things work together for good for those who love the Lord. I thought my heart would break four years ago when she decided to move out of our building and go to Indiana. She has two autistic sons, and they are a blessing. The middle son was like my own. His grandmother and I took him everywhere for years, getting him socially acclimated.

I was so upset I could see red. Thank God for my prayer, brothers. They reminded me of how I always preached to them about God being in control. I had to listen and agree. So, I changed my mind, thanked God, and blessed them before they relocated. Then God had mercy on me and allowed me to pray honestly for their success. Now, God has blessed her to be buying her own home. It pays to trust God! I pray these words inspire the soul to the glory of God.